Daring to Live

Ann,

It's hard to put into words how grateful I am for your love and friendship. God took a tragedy in our lives and gave us a bond, gift of a loving, soulful bond that I treasure greatly.

Thank you for trusting in me when life was in turmoil. Continue your own healing journey as you heal from this life. Challenges. Know that you are never alone and He is listening when you pray.

In love & friendship,
Michelle
9/2016

IN PRAISE OF *DARING TO LIVE*

These poems, so carefully crafted, are expressions that obviously come from both the mind and the heart. As we read and ponder on them, we can accompany Michelle on her journey of grief and in doing so find a helpful resource for our own journeys.

After significant losses in our lives, we naturally yearn for healing and wholeness, for the restoration of faith and hope. Michelle has given us a gift that will encourage us to be honest and transparent, and allow ourselves to grieve in healthy ways, and eventually move forward toward a confident future. We will also do others a special favor by sharing these writings with them.

Weeping may linger for the night, but joy comes with morning. Psalm 30:5

—Pastor Russell C. Lee

There are some unmistakable moments in life where God's handprints are a witness to his presence. Such was a moment when Michelle and I first met in 2010 while volunteering at a sporting event. Not only did we have the same last name, our husbands had died only months apart while riding their bicycles. We instantly became friends, and together we began our journey through tragic loss. Without reservation, I strongly endorse Daring to Live. It is a must read for anyone longing to grow "out of the darkness". Michelle's own photography and writings invite the reader to travel with her from the valleys of life to the mountaintops. There you will encounter the joy and peace of God like never before.

—Love you in deep faith. Sherry Anderson

Loss changes us. It can change us for the better, or the worse, but we cannot remain the way we were in the moments before the phone call or the knock on the door that announced the new shape of our world.

Michelle Anderson has written a beautiful testament to how the experience of loss and grieving that loss contribute to that change. We develop different priorities. We gain a new awareness, sensitivity, empathy. Eventually, we are able to recognize those changes and reach back to help others just beginning their own grief journey. Michelle's experience will reflect yours in some ways, and yet yours will be entirely unique.

My great thanks to Michelle for courageously sharing her journey and her hope, with all of us.

—Jade Richardson Bock, Executive Director, Children's Grief Center of New Mexico

---

Michelle created beautiful bereavement poetry from her heart and soul to share her personal journey of healing, letting go and moving on. Accepting, life continues even when our lives seem to stop. She guided us through the lonely pathway of the grieving process which explored giving permission to live again, keeping our memories as a warm place in our hearts and forgiveness. It speaks to my heart.

—Jodie Hart, LCSW

Daring to Live is a collection of poems the author began writing after the death of her husband. Throughout this collection, the author captures the spirit of the healing journey she embarked upon following her loss. Her poetry gently challenges others who are struggling with loss to set out on their own spiritual journey toward healing. For those who accept the challenge, she is a reassuring guide who personally accompanies her readers on their pathways to healing.

The book is divided into three sections. Each section represents phases of healing one can encounter along the spiritual journey. The poems do not gloss over or minimize the pain of loss, but instead, they encourage readers, little by little, to consider new attitudes and insights about their lives; about their losses. It is the author's hope that over time, readers will discover they are ready to ask the deeper question: How can one discover new meaning and purpose in life out of the pain of loss? Consider, for example, this passage from *Daring to Live:*

Look deep inside your heart
For answers to questions not yet asked

Only felt within your soul

Follow the unknown
Weightless like a feather in the wind

Trust what can be
If only you allow it to breathe

In addition, the author has included photographs in her book that invite readers to linger and reflect on their grief; to reflect on their unique reactions to the thoughts, feelings and images that are held within. The accompanying reflective word statement below each photograph encourages further introspection.

As a professional working with those who have encountered loss in their lives and who are struggling to discover new meaning and purpose in life, I will use this book, *Daring to Live,* in one-on-one short-term counseling sessions and in small group adult workshops to encourage others who are dealing with the pain of loss to gather their courage and launch out on their own spiritual journey toward healing.

—Linda H. Phelps, Ph.D., LMFT

When dreams are dashed and your inner mirror is shattered, Michelle's collection of thought provoking poems, reflections, and images can help repair and reconstruct that looking glass. Follow her as she rebuilds her life to promise after a sudden tragedy.

—Marcine Husman

Daring to Live

to Live

Loss as a Way of Awakening

MICHELLE M. ANDERSON

Daring to Live: Loss as a Way of Awakening
Copyright ©2016 Michelle M. Anderson

ISBN: 978-1-940769-55-4
Publisher: Mercury HeartLink
Printed in the United States of America

Cover and interior photographs
by the author.

Photograph of family p. 110
by Alexa and Dan Quinn

Michelle M. Anderson

daringtoliveblog.com

Mercury HeartLink
www.heartlink.com

Michelle M. Anderson

daringtoliveblog.com

DARING TO LIVE

SECTION ONE — LONELY

SECTION TWO — HOPEFUL

SECTION THREE — LIVING

SECTION FOUR — LOOKING AHEAD

KURT ROBERT ANDERSON—HUSBAND
1959-2010

My Darling, the pain of your death has not altogether faded, and I doubt it ever will. But with almost every passing day my unhappiness is translated into hope for a new beginning. Life is different and more demanding than it would have been had you lived, but I have been unbelievably blessed by your life having touched mine. I am intent on finding all the love, passion, and joy that you would wish me. Even as I write this I can feel you smiling down on me from heaven.

I am not certain where my life will lead me now. However, I do feel that if I continue to believe and trust in God, it will be revealed to me one brush stroke at a time, resulting in a masterpiece like I found in you!

I know that without God's support I would not be where I am today. I would be entangled in the remnants of the past, unhappy and longing for something I could never get back.

Instead I am thankful for what we shared together and hopeful that one day I will find a new love that will not diminish the love I have for you, but will be a new connection to happiness in the now presence of today.

I love and miss you still!

Gratitude: *Let me be thankful for the love and support of others in my life.*

As nature thanks spring for bringing new life, how are you thankful today?

ACKNOWLEDGEMENTS

Life is a journey; the journey is really what wrote this book. It is a collection of all the emotions experienced and gathered from moments in time that generated the words that flowed into poems that you are now reading. They just needed someone to capture them on paper, and that someone was me.

In order for me to accomplish this I needed all of you, my many friends and families who so graciously supported me and my boys after the loss of my husband Kurt, a loving man and tireless father. You gave me the confidence and the strength to live on, and this book of poems and images are a reflection of that journey.

It would not be just if I did not give my utmost thanks to my publisher, Stewart S. Warren of Mercury HeartLink, who took my vision and made it beautiful.

My life was forever blessed when I met my editor, Charlie McKee of Editors Proof, who took the time to get to know me before reading what I wrote. In doing so, her input and suggestions came from her heart.

I want to enthusiastically thank each of you, my good friends, who read my early drafts: Jean Haglund, Laura Tacker, Sherry Anderson, and Sheila Miller. I would like to give extra praise to Pastor Russell C. Lee, Michelle Baade, Patricia Lenzer, and Marcine Husman, who provided creative ideas that made my book what it is now.

Finally, I want to honor you, the reader, for having the strength and courage to face the challenges that have arisen from your own loss and to celebrate your willingness to dedicate the time to work on growing through your own grief journey.

Preface

Dear Reader,

I wrote this collection of poems and took these photographs as I grieved the loss of my husband, but now I am giving them to you.

It is maybe the week, month, year or more after your own loss. Let us be honest; it has been difficult. Changes have happened to you, and you are different now.

My hope is that, as you travel through each section of this book, you will find the motivation, support, and spiritual fuel you will need to continue working through your own grief. Grief is not limited to grieving for loss of life; it can also be a result of a loss of love, loss of confidence, loss of good health, loss of self-identity, and many other not-so-obvious losses, too.

My desire is to help you walk through your journey one day at a time. Letting you know through the different mediums of connecting—my words, images and reflective thinking—that you are not alone and there is hope for a renewed future.

The fact that you are reading this book lets me know that, like me, you want to be free to live again and create a healthy environment of love and encouragement for yourself and others in your life.

Is it going to be easy to do? No. Is it going to be worth the effort? Absolutely!

The organization of this book comes from my poem titled "Stages." It was not the first poem written, but led me to organize the poems I wrote to reflect the beginning, middle, and later stages one may experience when healing from a loss.

May you find a connection with one or more of these poems, images, and reflections, and may they bring you inspiration and hope.

Remember that you are on your own personal journey, but you do not have to do it alone. Look for those shepherds and support avenues in your life. If you do not have one, seek one out.

In Love and Friendship,

Michelle

STAGES

LONELY
Bare and Exposed to my surroundings
Feeling vulnerable and alone
Reaching out with all my strength
Trying to balance my self
Fearful of what will come
Afraid nothing will

HOPEFUL
Signs of new life ahead
Growing out of the darkness
Feeling stronger every day
Curious of what can be

LIVING
Life blossoms like the buds on a tree
Giving joy to each new day
A new future seems possible
I see it
Feel it
Dreams are alive
My spirit uplifted
Happiness is within reach

INTRODUCTION

Why poems? Why now? I started by writing a few poems for friends and family who had lost someone. The words just came to me. They were not planned, nor was I thinking that writing poetry would become an essential part of something I would need to do to make it through a day, a night or even a single moment in time.

But that's exactly what happened. I had written very few poems prior to June 30, 2010, when I lost my husband of seventeen years. Since that time they have been a vital part of my healing journey.

The grief progression is unique to each individual and you will travel at your own pace and in your own way. There is no "normal" length of time you will grieve. Some may say they were able to move on quickly, working through their loss in just a few months; others may say it took one, two or even more years.

Take the right length of time for you, whatever you need!

Many of my poems were written to express a feeling or to capture a snapshot in time. Others were written to provide hope to me, and now to you, that life would go on, get better, and that new happiness would be found along the way. A lot has happened in the years since my loss and these poems are a reflection of the emotional roller coasters I have ridden along the way—many alone, some with family, others with friends, and even a few with strangers.

As in most grief books, you will be told that the healing process is not simple and does not follow a guideline, but that you will flow in and out of the various stages throughout each day, week, month, and year.

Never be surprised at the complexity of emotions you can and will feel as a result of your healing journey.

This book contains four sections: Lonely, Hopeful, Living and Looking Ahead. Within each section you will find a collection of poems that I wrote, not in chronological order, but that convey a meaning or express a feeling or emotion that one may experience when grieving that fits best in that particular category. Dispersed throughout each section in between the poems are the photo images I took along my healing journey that are meant to do the same. Below each picture is a reflective word statement and related question for you to ponder as you move through the pages.

Following the first three sections are some additional questions regarding your thoughts, prayers, choices, and needs that may provide additional ways for you to foster growth and healing through written expression, either alone with your own thoughts and journaling or by using these to nourish discussion in a group setting. There are no wrong or right answers. Through your responses you are allowing yourself to nurture the relationships with the ones you love and see the possibilities that can take place in your life. I pray that these exercises will provide you optimism for a positive future.

It is your book now. I encourage you to utilize the empty spaces on the pages as your healing canvas to write your own feelings next to my words and images.

My goal is that these poems, images, and exercises will provide useful material that can be used alone or in conjunction with counseling, self-help groups, spiritual gatherings, and other sources of emotional support that you may be using. Use this material in whatever way works best in your life.

So let us agree to walk together page by page through the sections of this book. My deepest intention is to give you an initial boost of hope to keep you moving forward. Onward!

SECTION ONE

LONELY

Bare and Exposed
to my surroundings
Feeling vulnerable and alone
Reaching out with all my strength
Trying to balance my self
Fearful of what will come
Afraid nothing will

Guidance: *Help me along my journey to seek a variety of support groups that will help me heal.*

Being in nature can provide many sources of healing. Where and what would you like to explore today?

Faith, Love, Joy, Hope, Peace

May faith guide you through your grief

May love of your lost one be a source of your strength

May joy and laughter come to you each new day

May hopes and dreams of your future become clearer

May you find peace in your soul to forgive

GRIEF

A five letter word
Yet oh so complicated

Some say there are stages
Unique for all ages

I know firsthand
It's hard to comprehend

Painful days and nights so long
Never feeling like you belong

Thinking you are getting better
Until you read the last letter

Struggling through the hills and valleys
Thankful for the friendly rallies

Time continues to tick on by
So many tears you will cry

There are no magic guidelines to read
Nor a recipe for what you'll need

A period of disbelief will take place
Remember it takes time it is not a race

You'll need help along the way
He is listening when you pray

Never judging you for how you feel
He is here to help you heal

TAKEN

Taken too early from us

He was a husband, father, brother, son

A man of true passion
A Competitor
A Mentor
Lover
And Friend

Taken by our Creator
Lifted to freedom

He looks down from above
Surrounded by God's love

His life on earth finished
His soul replenished

Taken, but not forgotten

Light: *Give me the courage to see the light even during my darkest of days.*

What are some of your special qualities that allow you to shine your light through the darkness?

Heartache

I long for your touch
Days go by missing you so much

A memory of the past
A wish that did not last

I knew from the start
Nothing could tear our love apart

But now my dear
You are not here

I put on a good face and pretend
But my heart is broken and needs to mend

SHATTERED

Sadness so dark
That living seems too painful

Aching bones too weak
To offer even a whisper of hope

Stripped of all familiarity
Sacred innocence gone

Heart ripped in half
Draining all things you've known

Why now?
What now?
Why me?
Why him?

CRAZY

Feeling a little hazy
Endless thoughts driving me crazy

Searching for some inner peace
But pouring tears begin to release

I've fallen down on my knees
I'm begging you please

Take away some of my pain
Dry up my tears of rain

Togetherness: *Let me remember that I do not have to grieve on my own, that I have people who love me.*

The road may seem long and lonely, but it does not have to be traveled alone. With whom might you want to connect now?

ALONE

You wake up each day in a daze

Wishing you could turn back the clock

Wanting to make the last day perfect

One last hug goodbye

A loving kiss that would last forever

A whispered "I love you"

Then you realize they are not here

And all you want to do is disappear

BLINDED

Tears flowing down my face
Sitting in this empty space

Afraid of the pain I feel
Trying to reason this can't be real

Darkness creeps within my mind
Leaving me hopeless and blind

Endurance: *Give me the strength to take the extra steps in my healing when I think I've given all I've got!*

Help yourself to see how far you have come by writing down some of the steps you have taken to heal since your loss.

TIME

Days pass slowly by
When I think of you I still cry

So much was left unspoken
My heart is aching and broken

Not sure where I belong
Not feeling very strong

I loved you so dearly
I hope in time
I can see my future more clearly

DRAINED

Your emotions...
Like heavy stones weighing you down

Your energy...
Drained as dry as a desert wasteland

Lifeless living...
Empty days with no purpose

Are you there?
Can you hear me?
What now?
I am listening
Yet I hear nothing
I feel nothing

I'm thirsting for a sign
A spark
A light
A connection to what can be now

Show me the bridge
Help me take the walk
Carry me if I fall

SHADOWS

I live in the shadows

Remnants of our life together

Are scattered in pictures all around me

Reminders of times

Shared with one another

Desperately, wanting to make the memories last

I hold tightly to the past

Lost

Wandering, going nowhere
Replaying memories over and over

Wishing I could change the past
Wanting to make those feelings last

Hoping I'll wake up and it's only a dream
Realizing it's not and wanting to scream

Wrestling with the pain I feel
Not knowing how to deal

Searching for the life I had
Memories of the good and bad

Direction: *Let me see the healing pathways that exist for me during this time of change.*

Just as water carves changes in the sand, so can you try new things! It is okay to dream again, to wish for change. What do you need now?

BROKEN

Crying endless hours of tears
Scared of your inner fears

Loss of love
Loss of confidence
Loss of self-identity

Alone mind spinning
Fighting changes no one is winning

Hours tick slowly by
Reaching out for strength to try

Remembering times we've shared
Hoping my soul will be repaired

LIFE CHANGES

My life has changed
It's been rearranged

Pain surrounds me
Tears blind me

I'm scared of today
Fearful of tomorrow

I'm empty and alone
Waiting for you to telephone

I'm remembering the times we danced so long
Listening to our favorite song

I know my life will not be the same
You're not the one I want to blame

You've blessed me with your love
Please give me strength from above

Help me walk another mile
Let me remember your wonderful smile

I thank you, for sharing my life!

LOSS OF MY LOVED ONE

Turmoil and pain
One day here next day gone
"What ifs" tormenting my mind
Crying tears keep me blind

Darkness begins to creep in
A loneliness from within

Flashbacks of times gone by
Oh how I wish you did not die
Kindness shown from all who care
Pulling me out of my despair

Hope I need
Grateful I am
Scared of course
God please be my source

Shelter: *Provide me a safe place where I can heal.*

Don't confuse safe with hiding. Where will your next adventure take you? Where will your footprints be found?

LONELINESS

We all know that feeling of aloneness
That silence that speaks so loudly it hurts
Reminding you of all that is lost
Stealing your hopes
Stealing your dreams
Stealing your thirst for what can be
You sit waiting
Your mind spiraling
Going no where
Yet you're weary
Exhausted from worry
Afraid of your fears
So you hide in your own made misery
Not realizing you have a way out
The keys to your freedom
Reside in your soul
The choice is yours
There is happiness on the other side
A welcoming that makes you feel alive

GONE

I am gone

But I am here

No longer in my earthly body

Yet, my spirit is strong

I feel your pain

I know your struggles

Healing will take more time

Your soul has no clock

I WONDER

I wonder where my journey will lead

I ask God for help and even plead

> I plead for forgiveness
> I plead for guidance
> I plead for thankfulness
> I plead for happiness

I wonder if He hears my cries

> My cries for help in the middle of the night
> My cries for help for strength to fight
> My cries for help to make things right
> My cries for help to see the new daylight

I wonder if He has a plan for me

     A plan for me to chew on and swallow
     A plan that fills me up when I am hollow
     A plan that forces me not to wallow
     A plan that has a path for me to follow

I wonder...

Renewal: *Replenish the energy source within me to strengthen me for the journey ahead.*

A mountain lake provides energy and nourishment to the wildlife it supports each day. What physical or emotional sources are you using today to help you heal?

ON THE ROAD TO RECOVERY

Honor your feelings! Be kind to yourself! Believe in your future. Loss changes you, and you are different now. But happiness is near—just on the other side of your sorrow and doubt. It takes time to grieve your loss. Each step of your healing journey will bring you closer to finding peace and acceptance with your loss. Take it one moment, one day, at a time. Surround yourself with those who allow you to grieve at your own pace and in your own way.

Take a moment to walk with me through the following personal study section. Be patient. Allow others to help you along your journey. By sharing stories and even your tears, you let others know it is okay to talk about your loss with you. Make the time to explore and ask yourself these questions and to reflect openly about what and how you are feeling now.

My Poems: The poem that resonates with how I am feeling now is...

My Thoughts: As I reflect my loss, I am feeling...

My Prayers: Give me the strength to heal my loss both emotionally and spiritually by...

My Choices: This day, week, month I will focus on what I can do, not what I cannot do, which is...

My Needs: Give me the strength to trust the things I cannot change and to seek the help and guidance I need for those things I can change. The help I need is...

SECTION TWO

HOPEFUL

Signs of
New life ahead
Growing out of the darkness
Feeling stronger every day
Curious of what can be

Order: *Let me find balance and stability even as my life seems in turmoil. Some days will be harder than others.*

The energy you once had may be less for awhile. As you try to find balance, are there more things others could do to help you?

PATIENCE

I am dying on the inside
My emotions unbalanced

I'm struggling to keep my mind
From going into darkness

Darkness, a place of uneasiness
Breathing in fear
Feelings of doubt
Are overwhelming me

I'm searching for strength
Strength to lift my spirits
Strength to give me hope

Hope that happiness will emerge
One moment, one day at a time

Patience, my dear...

SAY SOMETHING

I need to tell you something
Not sure how or where to start

I want to thank you
For what you gave me all those years

A love that was unconditional,
Support that was not selfish

Care that was genuine
Hope that allowed me to dream

Security that made me feel safe
A heart that was not judgmental

Freedom to make mistakes
Without fear of disapproval

Healing

I know you are hurting and feel broken

Struggling to do what seemed simple not so long ago

Trust that you are not alone

That He is walking by your side

Ask Him for help

Fear not for He is always listening

He has prepared you for this

So tap your inner strength

Practice patience daily

Reward your progress

Embrace your courage

Celebrate the wonderful person

And friend you are to me and all of us

Remember you are not alone...

MY SOUL ACHES

My soul aches
My heart breaks

Memories begin to fade
Like the sun in the shade

Tears I've tried to hide inside
Instead flow like the ocean's tide

My emotions constantly flowing
Thoughts of you keep on growing

Feeling abandoned and out of control
The reality that you're gone has taken its toll

Faith: *Help me to believe in what I cannot see.*

Sometimes it is hard to have faith when you feel life has not been fair. Your emotions may be clouding your spiritual vision. How are you working to restore it?

PURPOSE

God's tasks
Handed down
Giving each soul a purpose

Delivering a message
From our Lord above

Sometimes they may seem
Trivial or unimportant
But trust they have a
Much deeper meaning

Don't question but
Follow the direction given
Embrace each task

Open your mind
To what can be
If you only trust
And believe

Ponder? Maybe
Dwell on it? No
Wonder? Absolutely

Become paralyzed?
No way

Thirst for His words
Found in scripture

Strive to live for others
So that they may see

The love of God
Working in you

Remember death is
Just a passage
"The best is yet to come"

Determination: *Give me the strength to move forward with my life and not give up in the face of challenges.*

Things may seem like they are piling up and up and up. What challenges are you faced with today? Can you turn them into opportunities for change and self-growth?

CHALLENGES

Our daily coping skills are challenged over and over

We wake up each day with the remnants of the past

Always puzzling our minds

While new challenges arrive each day

Keeping God in our presence is so essential

To allow Him to lighten this heavy load

And to share both the burdens and the joys!

Changes, But...

Wanting change
But fearing change

Wanting to move on
But scared to move on

Wanting to meet someone new
But not knowing what to do

Looking for a sign that says okay
But not knowing if it could be today

Trusting it will come one day
One day soon... I'll be OK

OH GOD

I hear your message

Slow down

Do less

Listen openly

Reflect with spirited eyes

Be grateful

Shine your light

CELEBRATE THEIR MEMORY

Celebrate each new day
Enjoy every sunrise and sunset
Laugh often
Elicit a smile in others
Be thankful
Reach out to help others
Always give freely
Take nothing for granted
End each day with a prayer

Another Day has come and gone
But my memories of _____
will always remain strong

Comfort: *Help me find safety and nurturing—not only in family and friends, but in my spiritual healing too.*

There is value in all experience; the pain of your loss will become less over time. You can learn to live around it. Ask yourself: what have I learned about myself so far?

A Shepherd

Goodness comes from those who care
Always helpful and willing to share
Lifting others out of despair
Helping you realize life is not always fair

Willing to provide a comforting hand
Or just listening to understand

Never judging who you are
Making you feel like a superstar
Lifting some burdens from your back
Protecting you from those who may attack

Never being far away
Providing you strength to live another day

I Am Here

I am here for you my child

Watching over you
Waiting for you to call

I so love you unconditionally

I know you are hurting
I know you are scared

And when you are ready
You'll not be scared

For I will give you peace!

Serenity: *Help me find calmness in my heart, no matter how chaotic my life seems.*

When was the last time you took a walk or a drive to marvel at the beauty that surrounds you? Plan it! Where to now?

I See

I see the beauty of life

In each sunrise

I see the love in life

When friends and family gather

I see the suffering in life

When someone you love has departed

I see the renewal of life

Each time the trees gain their
New leaves and flowers new blooms

I see the beauty in living life...

FAITH CALLING

It is our calling in faith

To give unselfishly

To be grateful

And to love unconditionally

It is only then, that we can receive

All that there is for us to share!

TRUST

He is there to hear your calling
To catch you when you are falling

Trust in Him with all your heart
Even when your world's falling apart

He is listening
He is watching
Don't be scared
He is prepared
Do not delay
Reach out today

Your healing can start now
Trust in him somehow

He knows you well
Trust Him!

REFLECTIONS

Sun setting on the ocean

Reflecting God's glory

A day complete
Full of His splendor

Yet twists and turns race through your mind
Triggering unanswered questions of every kind

Not knowing how you should feel
What is imagined and what is real

A picture imprinted in your mind
A hope for a future that you will find

Peace: *Help me find closure in the midst of all the uncertainties that have surfaced. Help me find peace.*

Just as each day ends in a sunset, bringing closure to the loss of a loved one can be peaceful, too. Take the time to write how grateful and thankful you are for your loved one now.

THANKFULNESS

Thank you Lord for this day

I listened to all You had to say

I know I need to try

To let my loved one go, to say goodbye

To celebrate times we shared together

Being thankful they'll be in our hearts forever!

HOPEFUL

We grieve our separate losses
Yet come together to share

Memories of the past and present

A safe place to be ourselves
Neither judging how we feel

Hours pass by
Touched by each moment
Learning about one another

Willing to take away some of the pain
Make a change or rearrange
One's day, house, or outlook for the better

Being a good listener
A person of comfort

Means
"Hope is renewed"

Growth: *Let me know that every day I am further ahead in my healing journey.*

Have you ventured out of the shadows into the light of day? How? Take a moment to go back through the pages and see how much you have grown.

On the Road to Discovery

I know you are thinking, "What now? Why me? How can I keep going? How can I make this pain and ache go away?" Well, I am here to tell you that you can. However, there is no way around your grief and no detour around the pain. The only way past it is through it — one day at a time. Gradually, you will be able to see the beauty in life again, and face your future with renewed hope and, yes, happiness.

Take a moment to walk with me through this next personal study section. Applaud each small step you take. Do not hesitate to give yourself a pat on the back or a high five! You do not have to go it alone; seek the company of folks who have been there. Support groups of people who have experienced similar losses can provide healing.

My Poems: The poem that captures my feelings and gives me hope is...

My Thoughts: I can learn through the pain of my loss by...

My Prayers: Give me hope to confidently trust your plan for my life by...

My Choices: This day, week, month I will choose to be patient with myself as I continue to grieve by...

My Needs: Give me the strength to ask for help and guidance from others each day in the following ways....

SECTION THREE

LIVING

Life blossoms
like the buds on a tree
Giving joy to each new day
A new future seems possible
I see it
Feel it
Dreams are alive
My spirit uplifted
Happiness is within reach

Awareness: *Give me the ability to be fully present and mindful of my surroundings as I heal.*

Sometimes we are so clouded with grief that we cannot see what is right in front of us. Is there anything new you want to discover?

OPENING

Doors open at times and we don't see them
Or we are unable to walk through them
Emotions, circumstances hold us back from

Being free

To experience what may be beyond the hinges of an

Opening

Passages filled with newness, wonder and joy
Should we choose to take the path set

Before Us!

What truly guides us toward or makes us turn away?
I have often wondered

But now...

I am willing to trust the unknown
That resides just past this Opening

COMMITMENT

I gave you this ring
A sign of our committed bond

It is a circle
With no beginning or end

It is a symbol of our endless love
One that will continue from me above

No more questions or asking why
I give you permission to fly

Our hearts will remain as one
Never to be undone

A new beginning for you is becoming clear
Go without fear, my dearest, my dear

SURVIVAL

Gone but not forgotten

Lost but still searching

Scared but not hiding

Wishing but not expecting

Laughing not crying

Smiling not frowning

Helping not hurting

Remembering not forgetting

Loving not hating

Giving not taking

Doing not waiting

Living not dying

A New Day

The Sun sets with colors of fire
Across the sky for us to admire

Rain drops begin to gently sprinkle
Stars light up the sky with each twinkle

Dancing clouds full of wonder
Help us to still remember

Joy: *Let me be open to experience love and happiness in my life again.*

Forming a new sense of happiness in your life takes effort. Name a few of your recent experiences that have brought you joy.

A RARE FIND

A gentle touch
A special caress

Memories of you do the rest

Life is precious yet
So unpredictable

Like a storm that blows into town

Whispers of what can be
Make things seem better

Open your heart

Get Ready
It is close
It is rare

It is special
A new connection

Untouchable

I long for the day

When I can stay

In your arms again

You are far away
But somehow very close

Unable to let go
But unable to hold on

My mind is wandering

My heart racing

More happiness seems near

If only you can let me go

Please let me go

Resilience: *Help me use the strength of my willpower to rise day after day after being knocked down.*

When I look at my own reflection, I am stronger today because of what factors?

Destiny Lives

Destiny surrounding my empty space
Spirits guiding me to a soulful place

What is waiting for me now?
My heart and soul must know somehow

Why does life seem so frail?
Endless obstacles marking my trail

Help me now to see and feel
That my future can be real

Tell me now which turns to make
Keep me genuine, never fake

VULNERABILITY

To allow oneself
To love unconditionally

To give oneself
Permission to live freely

Relinquishing all self control
Tearing down the boundaries

Set by ourselves and society
Barriers we build

To protect ourselves
From pain and hurt

Sadly they also
Prevent us from feeling joy
And happiness too many times

So why is it that some
Find it easy to love

Freely no matter
What the circumstances?

What unlocks their freedom
To love without fear?

Or is it the fear of not being
Loved that gives them
The ability to be vulnerable?

How can we trust
That the risk no matter
The outcome is worth taking?

That a moment of love
Is worth the pain should it be taken away

A Precious Gift

Life is a journey

A precious gift from God

One's ability to make a difference

Is revealed day by day

An indescribable feeling to live

In faith, trusting in each moment

Faithful: *Help me to remain steadfast in my faith.*

Trees learn to adapt to their changing environments. What avenues have you used to keep your faith alive and growing?

One Small Step

A journey begins with one small step, one new thought

Revelations of emotions are evoked as each second ticks by

Your mind races trying to keep up with all that is unfolding

Around you, within you, and yes, for you!

Whether alone or in the presence of others, things happen,

Changes take place,

And, yes, you are different as a result of them!

We wonder how, why, what for and often

Are left with no answers just more questions

The mystery of the inner soul intrigues me now

What does it need to survive? Thrive? And yes, grow?

Are any two alike, yet different?

And how did they come to endure?

What unlocks one's ability to believe, trust, give and receive?

Which empowers you more?

What is the greatest gift you will give yourself now?

Vision: *Let me see the beauty in my future through my eyes and feel it in my heart.*

The colors of the seasons provide pleasure for your sight. What have you felt that provides hope for your future?

BEAUTY OF NATURE

The beauty found in nature that surrounds us
Is just one of the ways God opens our minds.
He is giving us a glimpse of all that he has prepared for us

In order to see it you must be in the moment
Both with your spiritual eyes and with your soul
A soul not at rest will miss
The details of the message he has left for the day

Your spiritual soul is always hungry
Yet, at times you forget or become too busy to feed it.
You will soon realize your energy drained your focus foggy

It is then that you need to rejoice in His presence
Remembering the fulfillment He offers

Love Is...

Love is not always safe

Love is not always felt

Love is not always welcome

Love is not always received

Love is not always believed

Love is not always forever

But my love is...

MORE

You fill your day with an abundance of stuff

But realize in time it's not enough

You long for more to fill your heart

You're still unsure of where to start

A journey you know you must explore

The desire for more you can't ignore

You pray for guidance along the way

You're told to take it day by day

Magnificence: *Even in my sorrow, please give me the capacity to see the beauty in myself and my surroundings.*

The beauty of paradise is abundant on the shores of an island. How do you see yourself as beautiful?

GLORIOUS DAY

How glorious each day can be

When mind is clear and eyes can see

Help me to be thankful for what I receive

Block out the negative thoughts I may perceive

Help me see the beauty of your glory

Feel the blessings from your story

Lift my spirit to the sky

Remind me I will be with you when I die

Exploration: *Give me the desire to restore my spirit and resume my life again in healthy ways.*

Some trails are unmarked and hard to see if we are not open and willing to discover them. In what ways have you explored new or different physical or spiritual pathways?

ON THE ROAD TO LIVING LIFE FULLY AGAIN

Your healing journey begins with one new opening, one small step, one glorious day, and then another and another. The pain of your loss lessens over time but never really goes away completely. You will find that days will come when you are not so focused on the loss of your loved one—leaving space and time for new thoughts, dreams, activities, and people. Memories of your loved one will no longer make you sad but will warm your heart.

Take a moment to walk with me one final time. It is a true turning point in your grief when you are able to give up asking, "Why?" and instead ask "Now that this has happened, what shall I do?" This new question acknowledges that your life has been forever changed, but now you are open to what can be. Look back to the other sections, and see how much you have grown.

My Poems: The poem that provides me inspiration to soar again is...

My Thoughts: I can live my life fully now by...

My Prayers: Give me the wisdom to move ahead in my life each day by...

My Choices: This day, week, month I will relinquish my right to understand why and focus instead on what I shall do now. I shall start by...

My Needs: Give me the freedom to express the needs I have and move forward positively in my future. My needs now are...

SECTION FOUR

LOOKING AHEAD

Today you begin a new journey
One that seems a little scary
To discover your gifts
You must open your heart
In opening your heart
You may feel pain
Or instead pure joy
If you are honest
You will experience both

ARE YOU LIVING LIFE?

We are all gifted in one way or another
The key is to unlock the fruit of one's being
And live abundantly

Can one live without fear
And give fully as the sun gives to the earth?

Is it possible to relinquish one's self
To the surroundings
And reap more from one's life?

How do we let go
And walk without
The comforts of a safety net?

How do we believe in something
We cannot touch and
Have not seen with our own eyes?

What gives us the ability
To blindly trust in
What can be if only we can let go?

What allows us to
Leave the nest and soar?

Do the earth's tremors and quakes
Speak to us without our knowing?

Do rivers and streams that flow
Nourish our thirst for more?

Do the mountains we climb
Provide more than the challenge
Of the journey itself?

Do the stars in the sky
That twinkle ever so brightly

Give us the hope of something
More beyond what we can see?

Is it possible that we can learn
From the salmon
Who embrace dying as a passage to something more?

Or yet that of an ant
Who continually carries loads more than twice its size?

Can one change
Like a tree
Each season when it drops its leaves?

What truly gives us life each day and
Is it the same for all?

I think not

But let us be hunters and gatherers
Willing to feed others all we have harvested

Give until we have nothing left to give
Shed new life
Like a snake sheds its skin
Over and over and over

It is then when you may know you have lived life fully

Believe In The Future

I know you're hurting and afraid of the unknown
But one day you'll look back and realize you have grown
The days ahead will seem dark and long
Remain positive, your future is strong
Surround yourself with family and friends
Realizing inside, your heart is on the mend
Don't fear, for you are not alone
Stay away from those who may cast a stone
Look forward, your future is bright
Remember healing takes time and in time you'll be all right
Reach out and explore new goals
Don't be afraid to try new roles
A chapter is ending— look back with love
Embrace your future knowing there is help from above
Start now and do not delay
Your happiness begins with you today

Trust: *Instill in me the ability to trust in the unknown, to believe in what is now and to be open to what can be.*

It's tough to walk without a safety net towards something you cannot see. It takes believing in yourself, faith in God, and trusting in others to share in that journey.

BE STILL

Be still my friend

Let things naturally unfold

Be open to what comes your way

Let life breathe within your soul

Release what you fear

Tear down the walls you've built

Open doors you've closed

Unlock your heart

And listen from the inside

Love within the Soul

I live in the shadows of my soul
Seldom revealing the depth of my love
A place inside that is yearning for more
A spiritual awakening that is ready to grow

I desire to share this feeling
To be enlightened
Living fully in the moment
Ready to give and receive
The joy and peace that
Can be found when one
Is letting life unfold

Trust is an essential ingredient
A necessary piece to the puzzle
That allows one to believe in what can be
It takes faith, a willingness to relinquish control

To let go, to set free,

Those fears that reside within our minds

Daring: *Give me the freedom to take the next step, to look beyond the Opening to soar to new heights.*

Take this opportunity to ride a new wave, to explore a new you. What now, my friend?

DARING TO LIVE

Dangerous are the dark clouds that blind our vision
Those that keep us from growing keep us from living

Bright are the stars that can enlighten our future
Once we are open and clear the way

Precious are the thoughts that can nurture our soul
Unlocking the love which one can grow

May the beauty of each new day inspire you
In ways you thought not possible

Look deep inside your heart
For answers to questions not yet asked

Only felt within your soul

Follow the unknown
Weightless like a feather in the wind

Trusting what can be
If only you allow it to breathe

ONWARD!

Congratulations! You made it through another day and another and then another. These are victories: they are huge, honor them.

After a loss the "whys" will torment you, paralyze and confuse you, leaving you in a dark place all alone. Do not be surprised years later when anniversaries, birthdays, or special occasions bring back feelings of grief you thought you had long before laid to rest. It is not a matter of if this will happen; it is a matter of when.

Your own journey through grief will never be quite like that of another person; each of us is unique. Embracing grief can teach us how to live and how to love again. Every loss is significant. Loss is a normal part of life and cannot be avoided. We grow by working through the loss and accepting the loss. Be patient with your healing; it does not happen all at once. It is an evolution over time. Do not try to take shortcuts; many of the most useful lessons can be learned by making and taking all the stops along the way. Do not be in a hurry to get to the next destination; there may be more to learn by staying put longer where you are.

Experience as much as you can from a mindful place, without judgment of what is. Allow it to be as it is. Even in pain and sorrow one can find and experience joy, hope and thankfulness. The smallest of experiences can be more impactful and revealing than you realize. Take the time to treasure the moments you have.

Sad events are all part of our journey— not just tragic moments in time. It is through events like these that we are reminded and taught the value of our lives and of our loved ones with a deepness and passion we perhaps never could have imagined before.

Each time you read this book, may you find a powerful connection with one or more of the poems or images. And may this book provide you a positive healing foundation.

I encourage you to also explore various resources for healing along your journey. They do not have to be poetry or photography as it was for me. They can be different avenues such as: walking, talking, reading, meditating, painting, journaling, praying and many other creative outlets.

This book was for me in my healing process, and now it is for you in search of freedom to live life more fully after your loss. If you believe in the healing power of words and that "a picture is worth a thousand words," these poems and images are for those of us who are willing to trust the unknown that resides just past this Opening.

Thank you for allowing me to be your guide on this part of your journey.

Treasure yourself,

Michelle

A COLLABORATION OF ARTISTS

Slater Buron is an inspiring young artist newly discovering his artistic talents which span many mediums, from the beautiful illustrations found in *Daring To Live* to his work with oils, water colors and woodwork. As a sophomore in college he is beginning to explore where his talents will take him. I am excited to share in this part of his journey. His illustrations are found on pages 10, 42, 70, 96 and on the facing page.

My photo Images were inspired by my love of nature. I believe there are so many stories and emotions to be captured and told through the camera lens. I am glad I could share some of my experiences with you.

Looking Ahead by Slater Buron, 2016

ABOUT THE AUTHOR

MICHELLE MILLER ANDERSON and her then fiancé Kurt came to Albuquerque, New Mexico, as transplants in the summer of 1992 from the Midwest. Here they married and raised Kurt's son Kyle and their own two boys, Kasey and Karson.

In June 2010 tragedy struck, and Kurt passed away due to heart complications. Michelle discovered the writing of poetry and the use of photography as ways of healing through her grief. She continues to heal and grow through both spiritual and physical pathways, including tennis and Mindful Awareness Meditation. Her most valued and valuable role in life is as a mother to her three amazing boys.